it's okay not to be okay

it's okay not to be okay

A raw and honest guide to finding strength, healing, and *self-love* in a world that asks us to hide our scars and silence our *pain*.

GHANISHTA KHOSLA

AMARYLLIS
An imprint of Manjul Publishing House

AMARYLLIS

An imprint of Manjul Publishing House Pvt. Ltd.
• C-16, Sector 3, Noida, Uttar Pradesh 201 301, India
Website: www.manjulindia.com
Registered Office:
• 2nd Floor, Usha Preet Complex, 42 Malviya Nagar,
Bhopal 462 003 – India
Distribution Centres
Ahmedabad, Bengaluru, Chennai, Hyderabad,
Kochi, Kolkata, Mumbai, Noida, Pune

it's okay not to be okay by Ghanishta Khosla

This paperback edition first published in India in 2026
Third impression 2026

ISBN 978-93-7317-407-5

Printed and bound in India by Repro India Limited

To all those struggling with their mental health, this book is for you. I see you, I hear you, and I want you to know that it's okay not to be okay. Seek help when you need it, and never be ashamed of your journey.

Contents

*This book contains discussions of violence, trauma, abuse, gaslighting, mental health struggles, etc.

ONE

Teenage

THIS WAS PROBABLY THE MOST TERRIFYING PHASE OF my life, but I am grateful for it because it taught me to be the person I am today.

So, let's begin.

EARLY TEENAGE AND PUBERTY

This is when we experience changes both physically and mentally. Our bodies start to change. In my school, boys began seeing girls differently, and girls were taught to dress 'decently'.

Coming from a middle-class Punjabi family, things such as sex and consent were not discussed often. Until the age of 18, I couldn't fully understand what consent was or how to say no to someone. Not knowing what consent and bad touch meant, got me into some disgusting situations. This happened first in 6th grade, then in 9th grade, and again in 12th grade. The worst part was not being able to realise that I was being touched in the wrong way until I grew up.

I used to stay up all night, wondering what happened to me? Why didn't I say no? Why did he do that to me?

This is what a lack of sex education did to me and is probably doing to thousands of other children in this world. Innocent and unaware people are being molested. What could possibly be worse than this?

I'm not saying not having proper sex education was my parents' fault. It was the system's. All throughout school, I was taught all about trigonometry and the history of our country but not a single thing that would help me to survive in the real world.

The main problem is that talking about sex, physical relations, and consent has always been such a taboo that no one talks about. This can result in non-consensual relations or being touched inappropriately without your permission, which can damage and traumatise a person for life.

I believe that every person has a right to say no to what feels wrong and uncomfortable to them. **Say no to what makes you feel disgusted, guilty, or used and don't be afraid, hesitate or feel guilty for exercising your right**. I felt as though I had been violated. I felt as if my happiness, self-respect, and sense of worth had been taken from me. However, as I grew older, I came to realise that it was not my fault.

If you are someone who has suffered or faced this in life, I am sending my love and power to you for being so strong. I am sorry you had to go through it; you most certainly didn't deserve it. I hope you find justice and peace.

Always remember one thing: It's your body, your choice.

Let's talk about consent in relationships.

People with narcissistic tendencies often try and manipulate their partners into having sexual relationships with them in order to prove their love.

One of the most common phrase they use is, 'If you really loved or cared about me, you'd do this.'

When their partner hears this phrase, they don't think logically; instead, they believe what's best for their relationship, which leads them to do things that make them uncomfortable, but they feel compelled to do so in order to save their relationship.

Please know that you don't have to do anything uncomfortable to prove your love. If that person truly loves and respects you, they wouldn't ask you to do something uncomfortable in the first place.

Respect is more important than anything in a relationship, and if you're not getting it, you know it's time to leave.

SCHOOL LIFE

Welcome to 365 days of nightmare in my life.

I was in 8th grade when a new trend of carrying mobile phones to school had started. Every student who had one brought it; hiding it in bags, pockets, or wherever they could find a spot.

Foolishly following the trend, I took my brand-new iPhone to school but got caught by the strictest and rudest teacher

I have ever met in my life. During the day, the headmistress confiscated my phone and boy, did I panic. I was so clueless that I self-harmed in a cry for help. A teacher saw it and reported me, again. It's so funny to think about it now; I guess time and years of therapy do heal a person. Later that evening, my dad came home and was wondering where my phone was. I was terrified of how angry and disappointed he was going to be with me. But being the great person that he is, he and my lovely mom both understood the situation.

Now the main problem was returning to school after a week of suspension. It was really scary for me as an 8th grader. The moment I entered, everyone looked at me as if I was some sort of a criminal. I was constantly reminded of the incident until I changed schools. A senior came up to me and said, 'Ghanishta, you're the girl who cut herself, right?' which was followed by laughter, but I ignored her. What could I say when I was so broken at that point. Even the teachers would purposely target and scold me without any reason. They would call the parents of the students who hung out with me and advise them to stay away from me. But what did I do to deserve that? What did I do to deserve no friends? If anyone from that school is reading this, what was my fault? That I was naïve and got caught with a phone? I mean, that was all it took for you to torture me mentally until I left that school.

After all these years, I have not forgotten and forgiven (provided that they haven't apologised) anyone who bullied me in that school. Still, one lesson that I am grateful for is that I learned how to not give a fuck about anyone and vibe alone. I did have one or two people who didn't judge me and even if we're not in touch now, I'll forever be grateful for them. Thank you for being one of the good ones.

The only lesson that school taught me was that people will try to break you until you crumble down like a cookie, but the day you stop thinking about what they think, you will be stronger than ever.

Crucial reminders:

- You are stronger than you think.
- You are more powerful than their hate.
- You define yourself, not someone else's broken ego.
- Those who love you will always stand by you.

A NEW CHAPTER? MORE LIKE A NEW LIFE

After facing intense bullying and begging my parents a thousand times to change schools, they did. In 9th grade, I transferred to another school, and it turned out to be one of the best decisions of my life, even though I had to face a traumatic and abusive relationship. (Everything can't be sweet and lovely, right?)

This school did give me a new life. Funny how the tables turned. One school made me suicidal, but the other one gave me a fresh start. Even though there were some toxic people, I found people who were mine. I found a best friend for life.

To all those who were in 11th A with me, I love you guys!

After joining college though, I realised how much better my school life was. It had problems too, but real friends made everything feel easy. I'd often find myself laughing and smiling about something that happened three years ago. It's surprising how I went from a girl who hated school, to someone who wanted to go there willingly and happily with a smile.

After everything I've been through, the best lesson I've learned is that you can always start with a clean slate.

Remember the following:

- Your past doesn't define you or your future.
- Your future can be very different from your past.
- Do not let your past get in between your future.

Some people will always try to throw your past mistakes in your face, but if you have changed and learned from them, then those people are simply being judgemental and projecting their insecurities onto you.

I made foolish choices in my past and trusted incredibly wrong people, but even after all that, I got something out of it: the experience that will help my future self to avoid making the same mistakes I made when I was young.

TWO

Relationships

After a few months, when I changed schools, I met a guy who I thought 'was the one.' Well, he definitely was the one who tried to destroy me, manipulate me, and control me.

You know how you like it when your partner is all cute and possessive at the beginning of your relationship but after some time, they are just clearly controlling you? It stops feeling like love and more like an order which, if you do not obey, means losing your relationship. I mean, if my parents do not have an issue with the clothes I wear, then why the hell do you have a problem? Why should I sleep at the time you tell me to? Who the hell are you to decide which picture I should post or which one I shouldn't? I wish I could have said all these things to him when he controlled me. Such people often manipulate you to do what they want. If you have someone in your life who wishes to control every action you take, **let that person go**.

Trust me, girls and boys, there is a huge difference between caring for someone, and hanging around with someone who only thinks about themselves and how your actions will benefit them.

Always choose someone who loves you enough to express what they think is right for you, but trusts you enough to know that you'll make the right choice.

You know when you're hurt, and you're trying to explain that to the one who hurt you? After a while, you're convinced that you're the wrong one, and it's you who's apologising. Then, my friend, you've been gaslighted!

Remember that your feelings are important and valid. They should be heard and acknowledged without making you feel bad about feeling hurt.

Common phrases Gaslighters use:

- If you loved me, you'd do this.
- You're not making any sense.
- Why are you overreacting over such a small thing?
- Why are you being so paranoid?
- And yes, their favourite one, **you are crazy**.

People may get gaslighted because they are so emotionally invested in their relationship that they stop thinking logically and start thinking about how to save the relationship instead.

I have experienced gaslighting myself, so I can understand that feeling of hesitation, that feeling when you want to say you're being treated wrongly, but you don't so that the fight doesn't increase. Please know that you deserve someone who treats you with respect, acknowledges you, and makes you feel heard and seen. You don't deserve a narcissist who thinks they are right all the time and only favours their needs.

They take your voice away which made you stand up for yourself when you were wronged. They make you feel like you're nothing without them. Personally, all the pain and manipulation ended up with several migraines, panic attacks and hospital visits in my case. If you can relate to my experience, please save yourself from these people. It may seem difficult to let them go. Even when you try to leave, they will make up all kinds of excuses, constantly apologise and ask for a second chance, but these are just traps for you to get caught up in their toxicity all over again. So, remember that once you distance yourself completely, you will be proud and happier for making a courageous decision.

Remind yourself that:

- You deserve respect.
- You are worthy of love.
- You are enough.
- Only you can control your life.
- Most importantly, if you cry more times in a relationship than you smile, you must leave.

Remember, relationships are supposed to make you happy. Of course, there will be fights and tears, but if the love is respectful and genuine, it will overcome all those hurdles.

HEALTHY RELATIONSHIPS

Healthy relationships are built on a common understanding of trust, respect, mutual efforts and reassurance between partners.

These are some of the main components where effective communication always plays a key role.

Trust

When we are in a relationship, it's okay to get jealous and insecure. If you're like me and have faced many betrayals, you will tend to have trust issues, which is **okay**, too. It was challenging for me to trust someone and believe in love again. What helped me the most in this phase was communication. Whenever I would feel jealous or overthink a situation, I would talk to my partner and clear it out. Who understands your past and does not judge it? Who wants to love you so much that you heal from your past horrors? It is important to have an understanding partner, to whom you can open up and vent about your problems. With time, 100s of conversations, breakdowns over minor issues and efforts, I learned to believe in love again, and so can you.

Respect

We all know the importance of respect in any relationship, whether romantic, platonic, familial or parental. When we are respected, we feel heard and valued. During a fight, people can disrespect and hurt each other's feelings by voicing their personal experiences. But instead of calling each other names and disrespecting them, why can't we just talk? Sometimes, kindness can go a long way. You will realise how easily things can get cleared out without having a long fight with tears and yelling.

Efforts

The thing I hate about efforts is when people stop putting them in. All of us have experienced the feeling that our partners aren't the same as they were or vice versa. When people get comfortable, they tend to get a bit carefree and stop making the efforts they used to. However, there's nothing more beautiful than putting in the efforts and receiving it. If it makes you and the other person happy, then what's wrong with it? It keeps your relationship alive and does not let the sparkle die.

Reassurance

People who have trust issues and abandonment issues know how important getting reassurance is and how bad it feels when you don't get it. It's okay to ask for reassurance. What's wrong with wanting to know how much your partner loves you now and then? We know that you love us, but when the overthinking kicks in, all we need is reassurance and a little bit of extra love from your side. Is it too much to ask? People who need reassurance will love you to the moon and back if you reassure them that your effort can make their day. People who need reassurance can come off as needy and desperate, but that's not true; their traumatic experiences and repeated betrayal makes them want reassurance.

THERE'S MORE TO LIFE

Some people tend to make their relationship their whole world, which is wrong.

Your world is full of many things, such as your career, friends, and family, and your relationship is a big part of it, but not everything. I have realised there is so much more to life. Finding a partner is not everything, and you can be just as happy with yourself, friends, and family if not more.

Finding love is beautiful and can give you happiness you never imagined, but don't make it so important that you forget there are other things in life, too.

As we all know, too much of anything is bad, so balance your life carefully and spend time with people who love you because life can change within a heartbeat.

THREE

Mental Health and It's Importance

RECENT DATA CITES THAT GLOBALLY SPEAKING, ABOUT 1 in 7 people (nearly one billion people) live with a mental illness. Rates are higher in certain age groups, with 1 in 7 adolescents (aged 10-19) experiencing a mental illness or disorder.

While 1 in 5 people in America suffer from mental illnesses, about 15% of Indian adults require immediate intervention for the same, with anxiety and depression being the most commonly faced and challenging mental illness.

The rising number of Indians who take their lives each year is deep seated in the social issues, financial inequalities and distress, prolonged physical illnesses and mental disorders, along with extremely high academic pressures among students.

The understaffed mental health workforce and stigma that prevents people from seeking help when it is needed the most, are other recurring factors for the growing prevalence of mental illnesses.

THE TABOO OF MENTAL HEALTH

The stigma surrounding mental health has made people forget that, **mental health is just as important as physical health**. Just because you can't physically see the effects of a mental illness, does not mean it's not there. You don't know what's going on inside a person's mind, and by the time people figure out something's wrong, it's usually too late. That is when everyone wishes that they could have done something. So, it's totally okay to go to therapy. I don't even understand why there's so much stigma against it. Society is so fast in labelling people going to therapy as 'crazy', that so many of us avoid going, and sometimes things get so bad and out of control that they take the grave step of taking their own lives.

Even if you don't have a mental illness, it's okay to go to therapy. Think of it as a daily health check with your physician where you learn more about yourself, your emotions, and your mind.

People do not ignore their symptoms when their physical health gets worse. Why? Because they know that if they do, there will be serious consequences. Similarly, for your mental health, things can keep getting get worse if you don't seek help when needed.

I've heard so many times people saying things such as, 'That person looked so happy; why did they take their life?' because someone with depression can have a blooming career and a happy family but could be fighting some really dark demons inside their head. This is why we say, 'Don't judge a book by its cover.'

Reminders:

- Going to therapy is totally normal.
- Getting the help you need and when you need it the most, won't make you weak. It only makes you stronger.
- You'll thank yourself one day for getting help.
- You'll be proud of yourself when you get better.

DEPRESSION AND ANXIETY

As a student, I am familiar with the pressure of having a successful career or achieving straight A's and what it can do to your mental health. It breaks my heart when I hear about students losing their lives over a piece of paper. Of course, it may seem really important to them, that's because they are told the same thing over and over again, 'if you don't score well, your future will end,' 'If you don't crack this exam, you have no career option,' but that's so not true. No sheet of paper or test can decide your future, and no exam is worth killing yourself over. That's the system's problem; they make us feel that these exams are everything. In fact, they are just tests to see who can memorise things fast.

EVERYBODY IS CAPABLE

You can't expect someone who wants to be a dancer to fit in with people studying to become doctors. These students work so hard to crack various exams that most of the times they stop focusing on their well-being.

When I understood and realised the importance of mental health, one thing that really stood out to me was, 'If I am not happy, then what's even the point of it?' And if you really think about it, it's so important. If you are not doing something which makes you happy, why are you even doing it? For money? Yes, it is a big factor, but don't forget that you deserve to be happy, too. You deserve to do something that excites you about living your life, which gets you up and going in the morning, and makes your mind and heart feel at ease. Life is too short and if something costs you your mental peace, it's too expensive.

Let's talk about anxiety, the king of worrying.

That feeling when you just can't help but keep worrying all the time over the tiniest of things, events and details? Yes, I know it's the worst.

Pocket-therapy reminders:

Well, I have curated a list of things that help me calm myself down during anxiety. Feel free to try them, and I hope they work for you too.

- Going out in nature; away from the city noise and traffic and just sitting in Mother Earth's calm and beautiful nature has certainly calmed my nerves.
- Watching my comfort show on Netflix with my favourite snack (Peri–Peri fries).

- It can be spending time with your pet like I did, with my best friend, Coco.
- Writing, writing, and writing all my anxiety and worries away. (A little journalling can go a long way.)
- Going out (not clubbing) with my friends, eating good food, and having meaningful conversations can help more than you think.
- Giving myself a pep talk.

WHY THERAPY?

Why should one go to therapy? It's simple. When someone isn't physically well, they go to the doctor. That's the way it should be with our mental health. If you feel like your mind is not in a good state or you haven't been feeling well mentally lately, going to a therapist should be an option. I'm not saying it's your only option, but try and keep an open mind. Let's talk about people who need help but don't know they do. People who have faced traumatic experiences and have created a pattern of behaviour because of that traumatic event need to address those patterns in order to heal from that event and move forward from it. You know, sometimes you can totally forget a bad experience. Your heart forgets it, but your brain doesn't.

You don't even realise it because it's so deep in your subconscious mind that the tiny part which hasn't healed acts out in the old behavioural patterns. Even if you feel like a tiny part of you is still holding onto something from the past, get help and heal it. Get on with your life because it is going to be full of enriching experiences. That's how we learn. Let go of that one because it doesn't define you.

READ THIS WHEN…

Caution!

You're about to enter the motivation zone. This part will help you whenever you feel demotivated or discouraged. It will reassure you that everything's going to be alright one day.

Get ready to be motivated.

… You feel like you're not enough

Hey there, do not let anyone tell you that you're a lesser person. You can achieve great things, achieve your dreams, and make the best of it. **Look yourself in the mirror and remind yourself of who you are; you are an amazing person who deserves good things and, most importantly, is enough.** Self-love is the most important love. Start loving yourself and see how peaceful and fulfilling it is.

You are enough.

You are capable.

You are strong.

... You feel unmotivated

Listen to me. It's okay to feel this way; everyone feels it. You are not alone, but it's a terrible feeling, right? So, let me tell you how to get rid of it. Imagine what your dream is and how badly you want to achieve it; the sooner you do it, the better, right? Don't think about what the world's saying; it's your life and your dream. Start taking it one step at a time. Do something to get closer to it, even if it's a tiny step. It's okay. Even that step will matter a lot. Think about how proud you are going to be when you finally achieve it. Think about your other milestones and use them as fuel to get motivated. Remember, you can do it.

So, get up and start working.

... You feel like you can't do it

Hey you, it's your dream. If you can dream it, you can do it. If all the great achievers and billionaires had thought they couldn't do it and had given up, then they wouldn't be where they are right now. Don't believe the outside noise that is telling you, 'You can't do it.' Prove the haters wrong; prove yourself wrong. You can do it and you will. You just have to believe in yourself. Life's too short to not even try. Keep trying, and you won't even realise how close you have gotten to achieving your goal.

Believe in yourself and follow your dream passionately.

... You're beating yourself up over a person

I know how annoying and heart-shattering it is when someone you love, doesn't love you back. It feels that they are the only one you want. If not them, no one else, right? But why? Life's too short to waste that love over someone who does not value it can be emotionally draining. Love someone who loves you back with their whole heart. Don't forget that your parents did not raise you to be miserable over a person who's not worth it. You deserve someone who loves you with the same depth you love them.

Think about it: While you're busy loving someone who doesn't love you back, what if you miss out on the one who loves you deeper than the ocean?

... You're exhausted and need a break

Everyone gets a little tired of life sometimes, and taking a break for your well-being is okay. So, let's see what we can do. **You can always take a trip to nature, and enjoy the breathtaking views of the lush green hills.** The calm and quiet of nature will surely get you relaxed. But if you're someone who doesn't or can't get out of your house, I will plan the perfect day for you. First of all, close your Instagram. You will feel much more relaxed when you're not scrolling through and looking at other people's profiles. Now, get your favourite snacks, put on your favourite show or movie, tuck yourself in bed and watch it. Put on your favourite pyjamas and cuddle with your stuffed toy, or take a nap because what's better than taking rest when you're tired. Now draw yourself a long relaxing bath or take a shower. Use that brand new body gel and enjoy your **'me time'**. It helps me a lot, and I hope it helps you too.

... You feel full of emotions

I was someone who used to hide her emotions, keep it all inside, and fill herself up with emotions. When all those emotions would pile up, I would vomit at once, cry all night, and then wake up with a migraine the next morning. I'd vomit all day, and somewhere I realised how unhealthy it was, both mentally and physically. So, I did what I had to do. I stopped piling up my emotions, and started talking about my feelings to someone I trusted, and who would not judge me. I can't tell you how better it made me feel; it felt like a big pile of weight had been removed from my shoulders. All the anxiety started to fade away, and it was one of the best feelings ever.

So, talk about your feelings and let it all out. Because the more you keep it inside, the more it will harm you.

IT'S ALL IN YOUR HEAD

Coming to people who say, 'It's all in your head.' When someone says this to you, just know that person doesn't know anything about mental health.

Mental health is a real thing.

Sometimes, I don't understand why it's so hard for some people to understand that. Like, come on, people, just because you can't see it doesn't mean it doesn't exist.

How would you feel if you get physically injured and a person tells you, 'It's all in your head' or 'Just don't think about it'. It would not make sense, right? Well, that's how a person who has a mental illness feels when their pain is ridiculed; when their pain is not given any meaning or importance.

Never ever assume that you know what's happening in people's lives. It may look fancy and even appear happening from the outside, but you never know what demons they are fighting within their minds.

I like to think when a physical illness is not treated, the end result is death; whereas when a mental illness is not treated, it ends up in people taking their own lives.

So, it's high time we educate ourselves on the importance of mental health and make our mind a more peaceful place.

At least one step all of us can take from our side is to practise kindness.

Once, I got myself into a habit of checking comments under Instagram posts, and damn, the world is heartless. The world is full of racist, homophobic, and sexist people. I would look at some comments, be taken aback, and think, how can someone be so unkind? How can someone be so damn cruel? I mean, the worst part is those comment sections were full of people my age and to be honest, it's fucking shameful. Like, what part of the quote 'If you don't have anything nice to say, don't say anything at all', do people not understand? It's an impossible thought but I really wish one day the world can become a peaceful place for all the living beings.

FOUR

Leaving Home

Ever since I was a little girl, I have wanted to explore, be independent, and be strong enough to handle everything on my own. That's when I decided that after my school ends, I was going to leave my hometown, Delhi, and move to a foreign country to attend college. I was one of the many students who wanted to leave their homes and build a life in another country. However, I was having a discussion about the same with a dear friend, and she gave me some really good advice. She told me if I really want to move out of my home, I should start by changing cities as changing continents would a bigger challenge. I'm so glad to have taken her advice. So, instead of leaving India, I moved to Pune for my college, and that was an experience in itself.

Preparing myself

To be honest, before I left Delhi, I didn't imagine how hard it could be living away from my home, family, and friends. I always imagined that moving out would mean having a better life, and trust me when I say I couldn't be more wrong. Although everyone can have a different experience, mine was shitty. I wasn't prepared for the storm that was about to come in front of me, for all the hardships I had to face. I had no idea what my future was going to be like, so I left with a heavy heart, smiling, yet feeling overwhelmed. Even though my college has ended, and I'm back to the place where I've always belonged, Delhi, I still wish I had never gotten on that plane three years ago, but we can't change the past now, can we? All we can do is try to find something good in all our hardships. We can find and embrace all the lessons we learned and make sure not to repeat the mistakes we once made.

It all began

Upon landing at the Pune airport, I started second-guessing myself. Was it the right decision? Was it worth it? But I felt like I had no choice. I felt like I had to do this now. I still wish that among all these thoughts, a voice in my head would have said, 'You can still go back; you don't have to leave.' I would have listened to it.

Somehow, all of this didn't feel so real till the first day of college, when I had to spend a night alone in my hostel room. I was laying there, staring at the ceiling in the dark with tears dripping down my eyes; realising that **I made a big fucking mistake!**

It all hit me like a train, but it was too late. The fees were paid, everything was finalised, and now there was no looking back. I had to pull myself together and go through this.

The first year wasn't as bad. It was pretty good, to be honest. Well, it was the only good year. I had good friends and an amazing time with them. I'll forever be grateful to them and the time we spent together. Those, really, were the good days...

The downfall

After the first year of college, I moved out of my hostel and got a flat, thinking that there were no more restrictions. I could stay out as late as I wanted, and everything was going to be good. But I was wrong again and everything became dull; my friend circles changed, I stopped attending lectures, and I realised that, once again, things would get bad and I should tell someone. However, there was no one to talk to. No one got me. During this phase of my life, I felt really alone even though there were people around me. Have you ever felt like you're living your life on repeat? Each day is the same and nothing interesting is going on in your life. Well, every day felt like yesterday for a complete year, and it got exhausting. I tried my best to change it, but it just wasn't happening. Sometimes life is going to suck, and no matter how hard you try there's nothing that can be done about it.

When it became too much to handle, I decided to go back to my hometown for a few days, and there, I truly felt happiness again. I felt alive, and after such a long time, I felt like I was living my life and not just surviving it. This made me realise the importance of so many things. I know that building a career is really important, but don't let that process make you miss the joy of your life. Don't miss the little things in your life because one day, you'll wish that you could turn back time and live those moments again.

Time passed, and the beautiful fifteen-day holiday I spent in Delhi was about to come to an end. No one talks about how hard it is to board a flight to a place you know will make you feel alone, but I had no choice than to go back. So, I pulled myself together and reminded myself that it would all be over in just a few more months. I never realised how hard living alone could be till I was laying in my bed, with no one by my side, feeling like I wouldn't be able to make it through this. Each day was dreadful and scary, but I made it. Even though the crippling anxiety and depression I felt during that period still gives me nightmares sometimes, I made it, and I'm proud of myself for that.

The rat race

My college was over, and it was day 53 of my job hunt. So far, I had faced nothing but rejection and was extremely close to giving up. Staying up all night, applying to multiple jobs and never hearing back can be a pain in the ass; it was so frustrating.

(Dear HR managers, please have the decency to at least revert back to a candidate, it just takes a minute.)

It can demotivate you and make you feel like a failure; being a part of this rat race for a 9-5 corporate job can get to you, but don't let it. It can make you feel like you're good for nothing, but trust me, **even if you feel like giving up, don't!**

Trust the process; your time will come. After finally getting a job that had me doing so much work and paid me in breadcrumbs, I finally realised that the stress of a 9-5 job is not worth it. Going through so much frustration, hours of daily commute, the workload and tolerating your managers for what? Living on crumbs? Deteriorating your mental health isn't worth it at all. Having a stable income is good and even a dream for many, but if you are paying the price with your mental health don't stay in toxic environments. Instead find something that fits your mental well-being. Even if it doesn't pay as much as you'd hoped, if it makes you happy, you won't regret it.

Things I learned the hard way:

1. Every time you're alone, someone will not be there for you; sometimes all you have is yourself.
2. Just because you're working hard doesn't mean you'll get paid well.
3. Your first job can be your biggest nightmare and crush your dreams.
4. The world is a terrifying place; be alert and take care of yourself.
5. Not everyone who is sweet to you is your friend.
6. People change and best friends can turn into strangers.

FIVE

His Lies, My Truth

DEAR READER,

If you have experienced similar situations, please remember you are not alone. Seek support from trusted loved ones or professional sources when needed.

Healing is possible, and you deserve peace.

People say monsters don't exist. I used to believe that too, until I loved one.

I never understood why people stayed in relationships that caused them emotional and physical pain, until I was in one.

It all started when I was 19, dating someone I had known since the 11th grade. In the beginning, it was picture-perfect, but people can't fake their personalities forever.

Slowly, the red flags started to show. The little arrogance in his voice. The verbal abuse. The micro-cheating. I started to see the rage in his eyes. But for the sake of the relationship, I gave him the benefit of the doubt and ignored everything. This turned out to be the biggest mistake of my life.

Because what happened next would leave me with a trauma I never would have imagined.

There's a line abusers love to say: 'It won't happen again.' And guess what? It always happens again, and never stops until you take a stand for yourself.

So, if you ever find yourself in a situation where your partner causes you any kind of distress, pain, or harm: run.

When my ex-boyfriend laid his hand on me for the first time, I was numb. I didn't know what had happened.

I couldn't cry, I couldn't speak, I couldn't move.

Now, if you're wondering why he hit me? Well, I saw something fishy on his phone. And when I tried to take it, he slapped me.

Who knew catching a liar came with a free slap?

And when I confronted him? There was no apology.

Instead, the words that came out of his mouth were,

'You provoked me, Ghanishta.'

He lied to me. He cheated on me. He hit me.

But, sure, **I'm the problem?**

After I told him that I need to break up, the emotional manipulation started.

He cried. Apologised. Begged me to stay.

And I'm not proud of it, but I got manipulated. Not just this once, but countless times.

And you'll see just how deep the manipulation ran, as you read further.

He promised it wouldn't happen again. And I believed him.

But soon, over a petty fight, he did it again.

This time, it wasn't just a slap. He choked me until I couldn't breathe.

I still remember the way he bashed my head against the gearbox of his car. I thought I was going to die.

At this point, you're probably thinking, 'She must have left him for good this time.'

I wish.

I tried to, but he pulled me back in, over and over again.

I told myself I would leave the first time he hurt me.

Then the second. Then the third.

And suddenly, I wasn't counting anymore.

Why did I stay for so long?

Not because I loved him, but because I didn't love myself enough.

Sometime later, I had to travel out of Delhi for work with my family.

It was the last night of my trip, and I was having dinner with them when I got a phone call from a friend who saw my boyfriend cheating on me.

A normal reaction? Fury. Tears. Breaking down.

But sitting in a restaurant with my family, I couldn't react and had to pretend like everything was okay.

Like I was okay. (When I most definitely wasn't.)

That was the first time in my life that I forced myself not to cry.

The next day, I returned to Delhi and this time, my hand hit him first.

Of course, he beat me up brutally after that.

How dare I hit him for cheating on me multiple times and abusing me physically and emotionally?

After I loved him, right?

But I did break up with him for good this time.

I used to ask myself, why did this happen to me?

That man beat me till I fainted.

Molested me when I tried to leave.

Tried to trap me in his house.

The day he beat me till I fainted, I thought I wouldn't make it out alive.

So much for 'I'd never hurt you.'

I used to come back home and look at myself in the mirror, hating what I had become, trying to hide my scars with tears pouring down my face.

Because of him, I had to start therapy.

When in reality, he's the one who needed it.

The worst part? No one understood.

Sure, I could talk to people about it, but unless you've been through it, you can't understand.

This was, by far, the scariest, most terrifying time of my life.

And I wouldn't wish it on anyone.

It has been months since I last spoke to him.

And oh my god, life has never been better.

Things I miss about him (I don't):

- His four apologies and 400 lies.
- The scars and bruises he put on my body.
- His unmatched ability to make **everything** my fault.
- Being gaslit into thinking I was the problem.
- The bare minimum effort disguised as grand gestures.
- Wondering who he was texting at 2 a.m.
- Crying over someone who wouldn't cry if I vanished.
- Explaining basic human decency to a grown man.

To the readers:

If you see yourself in a situation like this, please leave. Remember this, if someone hits you or is aggressive with you, they don't deserve you. I know it feels hard. You believe you can fix them, but that's not your responsibility. And in the process of fixing them, you will lose yourself.

Love yourself enough to know that you deserve someone:

- Who protects your heart.
- Who gives you flowers, not bruises.
- Who is gentle with you.
- Who knows how to love you properly.

Sending you love and power.

SIX

You Tried to Break Me, That's Cute

After months of enduring the emotional abuse, physical violence and all that cheating, I was fucking tired of my life and only had one motive now. To heal and forget about all the bullshit that asshole put me through, but I knew it wasn't going to be easy. I had nights full of anxiety, rotting on the floor, and just full–blown panic attacks, but to my surprise, the day I stopped talking to him was the last day I cried.

Shocking, isn't it? I realised I had cried so much during the time I spent with him, I was all out of tears. Suddenly, I didn't wake up with a heavy heart. I wasn't staying up all night wondering why someone's son did this to me. Life started to feel good again and I felt like I had been out of a prison; one that was killing me day by day. One morning, I caught myself dancing in my room to an old song I used to love. That's when I knew I was coming back to life.

That's when I realised, **no contact** is the fucking key. When I blocked him, I didn't just block him, but all the negativity and toxicity he was bringing into my life. With him, all of that went away too.

There was a time when I didn't realise my worth. It took a lot of self-love, pep talks, and breakdowns to help me realise everything. A big thank you to the people in my life who stood by me through all the dark times.

So many people don't cut off ties with their abusers, because the fear of their abusers finding someone else and never come back is scary.

How about you find someone else? Someone who is kind, calm, peaceful and honest. Someone who doesn't make you doubt yourself. You have your whole life in front of you; don't let it waste over someone who doesn't even deserve a fraction of it. You didn't come into this world to be someone's punching bag. You have so much to live for: your family, your career, your friends, and most importantly, yourself.

Change the narrative. It's about you, not them. Choose yourself.

Understand that the only reason you are not able to let go of them, knowing fully well that they are bad for you, is because you have developed a habit, a toxic pattern which will break you down eventually. You need to break out of that trap, no matter how tough it gets and be strong for yourself. The demon sitting in your head saying that 'one conversation can't hurt' is your worst enemy; kill it. You'll thank yourself later.

The happiness and peace I felt after deciding to go no-contact were priceless.

Going no contact was easy for me because I did a few things to take my mind off to a peaceful place, like:

- Going on long walks with a friend and letting it all out. (Talk about it till there's nothing left to say.)
- Making the gym my new best friend.
- Doing the things I loved, once again. (Think, is there something you love but haven't done in a while? This is a sign.)
- Spending time with my family. (I'll always be grateful for them.)
- Starting to focus on my future, and what I wanted to do.

Going no contact wasn't just about getting over him, it was about remembering who I was before he convinced me I was too much, too loud, too emotional. It helped me realised that I wasn't too much, he was just never enough.

If you're still stuck in such a cycle, know that you're not crazy, dramatic, or unlovable. You're just caught in a story that was never meant to be yours.

Rewrite it!

Remember that you deserve a love that brings you peace and happiness, not someone who makes you feel as if you are not enough. Remember to be kind to yourself, because if you aren't, how do you expect the world to be kind to you?

SEVEN

The Aftermath

BECAUSE SURVIVING IS JUST THE BEGINNING...

TRIGGERS I DIDN'T SEE COMING

While the relationship ended, the trauma lingered. The nightmares were still there, there were days when I could feel the slap or the way he choked me. I realised I had become more sensitive; whenever someone would raise their voice, it would scare the hell out of me. Sudden movements would result in me flinching, it wasn't easy at all. A door slamming too hard? My whole body would freeze.

I hated how weak I felt.

I wanted to stop feeling like a victim of abuse; I wanted to stop feeling like his victim, so that's what I did.

I changed the damn narrative.

I stopped thinking of myself as a victim, and started thinking of myself as a survivor of abuse, someone who survived a series of physically and emotionally traumatic incidents. Not just someone who had made it through, but someone who

rose out of it. Like a phoenix from the ashes. These incidents didn't make me weak, they made me strong. The fact that I made it out alive, shows how strong I was.

Don't let anyone disrespect you so much that you stop respecting yourself.

Your self-respect and self-love are your power; never let anyone take it away from you.

CLOSURE IS A SCAM

'I talked to them because I wanted closure.' If you've ever said something like this or heard it, then let me tell you one thing with love.

Dear reader, closure is a scam.

They knew **exactly** what they were doing.

They knew when they were lying.

They knew when they were cheating.

They knew when they ignored your tears and made you feel like you were **too much** for wanting the bare minimum.

They knew. And they still did it.

Not because you were unlovable. But because they **never cared enough** not to hurt you.

So now, what are you hoping for in this so-called 'closure'?

That they'll suddenly develop a conscience?

That they'll sit across from you and magically feel sorry?

That hearing them say 'I'm sorry' will wipe out the nights you cried yourself to sleep?

Will one fake apology make up for the pain they caused you? The nights you stayed up wondering why you weren't enough?

Let me break it to you gently,

Closure doesn't come from them. It comes from you.

You don't need to hear **why** they did it.

You don't need to sit through another explanation that's going to sound like a poorly written script filled with 'I didn't mean to' and 'I was going through a lot.'

You already know all you need to know: they chose to hurt you, again and again.

And that's the only truth you need to close that door.

If their words never matched their actions before, what makes you think **now** will be any different?

Stop looking for peace in the hands of the person who shattered you.

The closure you're chasing won't come from them.

It'll come the day you decide to stop reopening a wound just to see if it still bleeds.

It'll come when you choose yourself, fiercely, unapologetically.

It'll come when you walk away without needing them to validate your pain.

And one day, when someone asks you,

'Did you ever get closure?'

You'll smile and say,

'Yes. I gave it to myself.'

THINGS I'LL NEVER TOLERATE AGAIN

Once I survived hell, my standards changed. Before hitting rock bottom, I saw every red flag that led there, and after spending months there, I don't want to go back, ever again. So, to protect my peace, I started doing a few things (you should too!)

I have stopped tolerating '**almost**', '**maybe**', and **'I'm just not ready'**.

I have stopped accepting the bare minimum masked as effort.

I stopped mistaking mixed signals for mystery and silence for safety.

Because now I know better.

I've been through worse and made it out alive.

So, here's my new rulebook; written in scars, and with self-respect:

1. I'll never tolerate love that makes me question my worth. If I have to beg for affection, attention, or commitment, it's not love. It's emotional starvation dressed up as romance.
2. I'll never excuse disrespect just because I'm in love. I will no longer tolerate their anger and disrespect out of love or for the sake of the relationship. Love doesn't hurt. Manipulation does. Gaslighting does. Being treated like an option when I made someone a priority. Never again.
3. I'm never going to be someone's punching bag, where they dump their emotions. People need to realise the difference between venting out and hurting someone. Just because you are going through a tough time, doesn't give you the right to hurt another person.
4. I'll never stay in a place where I feel unsafe. Emotionally, physically, and spiritually. If being around someone makes me shrink, walk on eggshells, or question reality, I'm out.
5. I'll never downplay my needs to make someone else comfortable. I'm not 'too emotional'. I just refuse to accept numbness. I'm not 'too intense'. I love deeply, and I deserve someone who can hold that.
6. I'll never ignore red flags just because I'm lonely. The temporary comfort isn't worth the permanent damage. I've learned that the hard way. Now, I choose peace over chaos **every single time**.
7. I'll never wait to be chosen again. I'm not standing in line to be someone's 'maybe'. I'm the damn prize. If they can't see that, I'll gladly remove myself.

8. I'll never apologise for having boundaries. If someone sees your standards as a threat, that's their insecurity talking, not your problem.

After everything I've been through, I finally understand:

I am not hard to love. I was just loving people who didn't know how to love me right.

And now, I'll never let myself be in rooms, relationships, or realities where I have to fight to be heard, seen, or respected.

I've earned my peace. And I'm not letting anyone take it away from me again.

Dear reader,

Protect your peace, it's more valuable than you think it is.

EIGHT

Letters I Never Sent

To my abuser

You.

You tried to break me, bring me down to nothing, make me feel like I deserved the pain. But guess what? Every time you beat me up to flaunt your little ego, I only became stronger.

I don't know what turned you into a monster, (and frankly, I couldn't care less) but just because you had a shitty life, doesn't give you the right to try and destroy someone else's. You made me believe I was hard to love, but in reality, you were just incapable of love.

And even when I was crawling through the mess you left behind, you still thought I'd come back.

But I didn't.

I rose.

And while you're still busy blaming the world for your darkness, I've been busy finding my light.

Honestly, you lost a gem, and I'm so glad you did. (You never deserved me anyway.)

If I could, I would return to the night we met, not so I could relive it but to walk away before I even said hello.

You hurt me in ways I'll never forget but I'm learning to forgive you, and deep down, I hope you heal too.

Dear reader

If you have ever experienced any type of physical or emotional abuse. I'm so sorry, but you need to hear this.

You didn't deserve any of it.

Not one slap. Not one lie. Not one moment of fear, confusion, or heartbreak.

Let's make one thing absolutely clear:

We didn't cause the abuse. They did.

We didn't invite the trauma. We survived it.

It's hard to wrap your head around how someone's cruelty, when all you did was love them. And it's even harder when you're a good person with a good heart, because it makes no sense. You start questioning yourself: Was it me? Did I let it happen? Was I too blind, too forgiving, too loyal?

But here's the truth, and I need you to hold on to this:

Good people don't deserve pain just because they have big hearts.

We are not naive. We are loving.

We are not weak. We are trusting.

We are not stupid. We are hopeful.

And none of these things gave them the right to break us.

But here's what else is true:

We made it out.

What we went through was unfair. Cruel. Unjust.

But what are we becoming because of it? That's unstoppable.

So, to every person who's ever been called crazy, dramatic, or too much. Let me tell you something: You are not too much. You were just with someone who was never enough.

Keep healing. Keep rising.

Because one day, your peace will be louder than their chaos combined.

To my younger self

First of all, I would like to apologise to you.

I'm so sorry for the shit I put you through, you didn't deserve any of it baby.

Sometimes, I feel like I have failed you after what I put you through, but I promise you, I'm working hard every day to give you the life we dreamed of.

I'm so sorry.

I'm sorry for every moment you felt alone, scared, or unloved.

I'm sorry for the nights you cried silently, wondering what you did to deserve the pain.

You deserved to be safe. You deserved to be held. You deserved kindness, not chaos.

I wish I could go back and hold you. I wish I could whisper to you,

'None of this is your fault.'

You were never too sensitive. Never too dramatic.

You were just a little girl trying to survive a world that kept hurting her.

But here's the part I want you to hold close

I never stopped fighting for you.

It was for you every step I've taken, every tear I've shed, every piece of healing I've stitched into my skin.

So that one day, you could look around and feel **free**.

I'm building the life you used to dream about.

Slowly. Carefully. Honestly.

A life full of real love, peace, and safety.

A life where you don't have to shrink to be loved.

Where your softness is not a weakness, but your superpower.

You're no longer that scared little girl who had to face bullies and get slut-shamed when she was just in 8th grade.

You've grown into someone fierce, someone kind, someone unbreakable.

And I promise you, I'll spend the rest of my life protecting you in all the ways no one ever did.

We're safe now.

And we're going to be okay.

With all my love,

You, but stronger.

To my future self

When you read this, I hope you're sitting on a beach in Spain with the love of your life, thinking how far you've come.

You made it through things I never thought we'd survive. And I'm so damn proud of you.

We survived:

- Being abused (in every way possible) by a walking red flag.
- A ton of fake friendships.
- Some unfortunate situations because some people don't understand consent.
- Three years of college and living away from home.
- The death of my best friend.
- Getting bullied and slut-shamed by my seniors and some 'teachers' when I was merely 13 years old.
- The corporate rat race and toxic micromanaging bosses.

Right now, I'm healing. I'm learning to let go of the pain, the people, and the patterns that almost broke me. I cry sometimes. I get tired. I am working hard to make our dreams come true, but I haven't given up on us, not once. And if I'd remember everything, I'd never move forward.

I hope by now, you've created the life we used to dream of—the books, the freedom, the love, and the peace. I'm working hard for you. Every decision I make today, even the scary ones, is for your peace tomorrow.

Please don't forget how far we've come. Don't settle. Don't shrink. Don't love people halfway. Keep choosing peace. Keep choosing your worth.

Whatever you're facing now, I trust you. You've survived storms and turned pain into power. You are strong, but you don't have to be strong all the time. I love you, and I'm rooting for you always.

Love,

The version of you who is healing, hoping, and building the life you're living now.

To Ghanishta who stayed

Hey, sweetheart. How have you been? It's been a while, hasn't it?

When I last saw you girl, you were a mess.

Honestly, I didn't think you would make it out alive. I don't mean to be harsh, but what did you get yourself into? You deserved so much better, my love. What you went through, no one deserves that. I'm sorry you had to face that. You are as bright as the sun, your smile can make flowers blossom.

I'm sorry I took that smile away. I promise it won't happen again.

Those long, painful nights filled with crippling anxiety, which felt like they would last forever… are gone now, my love.

You are safe now… we are safe now.

To be honest, sometimes I get furious at you for staying with him after enduring so much pain… but then I think, it wasn't your fault.

You were just a girl in love; it was he who couldn't value you, but it's okay. I never needed him to value you; **I just wanted you to value yourself.**

Everything you went through is over now. No one can hurt us again like that.

No one can hurt you now. No one will. Not while I'm here.

Love,

The woman who rose for you.

The woman you became.

THE HEALING PROCESS

Healing is like stitching a wound without anaesthesia. It hurts like a bitch, but that's the only way to stop the bleeding. You know you have to do it, but remember the only way to heal is to remove the toxicity first, then the other ways follow. You can't keep sipping alcohol and still expect yourself to be sober.

That's why going no contact is the first step of healing. If you've successfully done that, you are already so much stronger than you think. The next step is self-control, because 99 out of 100 times, your abuser is going to text you, call you, or beg you for your forgiveness. What are you going to do at that moment? Are you going to get manipulated by old ways and fall back? Or are you going to choose yourself, and your self-respect? The choice is yours. One is highly fatal and will likely make you feel ashamed, hurt, anxious, and the other will help you find yourself. So, make smart choices because they will not change, but the consequences may be worse for all you know. Leave and don't look back, for your own good.

READERS WHO ARE STILL WAITING

If you're still crying over someone who made you feel like you were hard to love, know that one day, someone will come and love you in a way that makes healing feel like breathing.

One day, your heart won't feel as heavy.

One day, you will go to sleep and feel like the luckiest person on earth.

One day, life won't seem as hard.

One day, you will find the one whose love has the power to move mountains.

Trust me, you will love again. And it will feel like the softest sunrise. Wait for it.

NINE

We Don't Talk Anymore, and That's Okay

FRIENDSHIPS.

Something that shouldn't be complicated at all, yet somehow... they are.

They can be the most beautiful bond or the most emotionally draining experience.

In the last few years of my life, I've made and lost many friends, some of whom I still miss to this day.

Let me ask you something.

Have you ever had a friend for whom you gave everything—your time, your energy, your loyalty, but every time you fought, the blame was placed on **you**?

If yes, I feel you.

It's frustrating when you know deep down it's not your fault, yet you're the one always apologising, just to 'save' the friendship.

I've asked myself this so many times: 'Why am I apologising when I did nothing wrong?'

It sucks. I've been there. It happens to the best of us.

I once had a best friend who fought with me because I didn't want her hanging out with a guy who had slut-shamed and verbally abused me.

And her response?

'He wronged you, not me. Why should I stop talking to him?'

I ended up apologising. For peace, for the sake of our friendship.

But looking back... where was the friendship in that?

I tolerated a lot of disrespect and one-sided efforts in that friendship. Even when I moved away from my home, all alone; I was the one who had to put in all the efforts to maintain the damn friendship when that person didn't even care about my absence.

One thing that stuck with me is that people can be really selfish sometimes. They will be friends with you until you are benefitting them in some way and the moment you are not, poof, the friendship's gone.

Here's the truth:

Always being the bigger person will cost you your peace and your self-respect.

You think you're doing the right thing. You think you're saving the connection.

But really, you're slowly giving pieces of yourself away. And by the time you realise it, you're empty.

Just like any relationship, friendship requires effort.

It requires care, time, and most importantly, understanding.

A real friend won't need an explanation to get you.

They'll just know.

Lessons I've learned about friendships:

- Some people become friends with you out of loneliness. (Be careful, they'll leave the moment someone else fills that void.)
- After college, you'll realise how golden your school friendships truly were.
- Some friends secretly envy your growth.
- The people who care about you will always stand by you, even when you try to push them away.
- Childhood friends? They're treasures. Keep them close.

TEN

The One That Keeps You Up at Night

No, I'm not talking about a person or a relationship.

I'm talking about something else that's actually worth keeping you up at night:

Your future. Your career.

I say, **'I love writing. I want to be a full-time writer.'**

But society, my parents, everyone around me says,

'Writing is a hobby. How will you earn money?'

'What about a stable income?'

If you're someone in a creative field, I think you'll understand what I'm saying.

Whenever someone asks me, **'What do you do for a living?'**

I honestly have no answer.

And I'm a little ashamed to admit that, but it's the truth.

It's not like I didn't try.

I tried working the 9-5 jobs.

But some things just aren't meant for everyone.

I couldn't handle it.

The toxic, micromanaging boss.

The rude, entitled clients.

Working my ass off for six days a week and being compensated in breadcrumbs.

I was exhausted. And I quit.

Sometimes I wonder,

What would my life be like if I hadn't quit?

Would I have a stable income?

Probably.

Would I be happier? Have a peace of mind?

Hell no.

Am I scared for my future?

Yes.

Do I regret quitting my toxic job?

Not for a second.

Because I've realised something,

It's better to take time, to figure out what **you** actually want to do than to lose yourself in this rat race.

Yes, money matters. Yes, we all need to survive.

But you shouldn't have to destroy your spirit in the process.

You shouldn't have to sacrifice **who you are** just to earn a living.

So, to the one who stays up at night, wondering what are they really doing with their life,

You're not alone.

Take your time.

You'll figure it out.

And when you do, make sure it's something that doesn't cost you—you.

ELEVEN

Dear Future Writers, This One's for You

If you're an aspiring author, this one's for you.

Let me tell you about my writing journey.

I wrote my first piece in 9th grade. It was about kindness and got published in my school magazine. (You'll find it in the next chapter.)

Back then, I had no idea that writing would one day become **my everything**.

After that, I simply posted my thoughts on social media, little write-ups, straight from the heart.

By the time I reached 11th grade, I discovered anthologies, books that compile pieces from multiple authors. I started submitting my work and co-authored around 4-5 anthologies.

But at that point, writing was still **just a hobby**, a way to express myself.

I never thought I'd write an entire book. Ever.

Then came college. I moved to Pune, still clueless about what I wanted to do with my life, but I kept writing. One day, I showed a few of my write-ups to a professor.

The way he praised my work gave me the confidence I'd never felt before.

I still remember the goosebumps when he asked me to read one of my pieces aloud in class, and how everyone clapped. That moment… it lit a fire in me.

Months passed. I was still in Pune, still feeling lost, still 1.5 years away from graduating.

But I felt this constant emptiness, like I hadn't achieved anything. I was exhausted, lonely, and angry.

And that's when I decided: **I'm going to write a book.**

People didn't take me seriously.

But guess what? I didn't care.

Because I believed in myself. And that's all I needed.

So, I started my journey as an author, and I'm so glad I did.

When I was younger, I dreamt of being in the fashion industry. Never in my wildest dreams did I think I'd become a published author.

But life is unpredictable. It changes in a heartbeat. And sometimes, that change leads you right where you were meant to be.

If you're a writer, here's the one piece of advice I want to give you:

Be yourself.

Be raw.

Be honest.

Use your words to express **your** truth.

Don't wait for the 'perfect' time to start. That time doesn't exist.

Start now. Right now.

There's no time better than the present.

And whatever you do, **don't let people's opinions hold you back.**

Your story matters.

Your words matter.

You matter.

Be yourself. You won't regret it.

TWELVE

My Write-Ups

THESE ARE SOME WRITE-UPS BY ME. I WROTE THEM when I felt too overwhelmed and needed to declutter my mind. Some are motivating; some show my deepest and darkest thoughts. Either way, I hope they make you feel heard. You are not alone in this race called **life**.

The worst type of depression

The worst of depression is not the permanent one

It's the one that comes and goes

like waves

One day, you're happily going out with your friends,

But the next day, you're lying in bed thinking wouldn't it be so much better if you didn't exist

One day, you feel like you couldn't be happier

But the very same day, you've locked yourself in your room, crying so hard yet being silent about it, so no one hears

because even if they did,

You know they wouldn't get it.

Apology letter to my inner child

I'm sorry,

I'm sorry I'm not everything I thought I'd be

I'm sorry I couldn't fulfil your dreams

I'm sorry I made you cry so many times

I'm sorry for not being perfect

I'm sorry for filling your heart up with insecurities and pain

I promise you, one day, it will all be okay.

how did I get here?

from being someone so full of dreams and hope to just being on the verge of giving up?

where did it all go wrong?

when did I get stuck in this mess?

how did I go from being passionate and ambitious for my dreams to someone barely living her life?

I mean, life isn't that bad, but I know it could be better, much, much better, but when?

It's not like I'm not trying, I am, that's all I've been doing, in fact, I just keep trying,

Why? Where does that hard work go?

I promised myself when I was younger that I'd have everything I want when I grew up.

But look at me now, all grown up, but where's the life I wanted?

Maybe not today, not tomorrow, not even a month,

but one day, I will get the life I want.

18 important lessons I've learned:

1. Don't think or worry about what others say about you. You live only once, so why waste time thinking about what others say or think about you?
2. Choose people who choose you. Life is too short to love people who don't love you back. It'll hurt, but let go of the people who don't value you.
3. It's never too late to start doing what you love. What's the meaning of life, if you aren't doing what you love?
4. Don't love someone more than yourself because they can leave or hurt you. You only have yourself at the end of the day.
5. Stop thinking about the past; you can't change it.
6. Stop worrying about the future; you can't control it.
7. It's okay to let go of people. It will hurt you now, but you'll be happy that you did it.
8. It's harder to move on from someone you didn't date, than from someone you were in a relationship with.
9. Not everyone you fall for is meant for you; what's meant for you will find you.
10. Go buy that thing you've been looking at forever. Life's too short. Don't go with regrets.
11. If you were born without that person, you can most certainly live without them.
12. Making a career is important, but taking time out for yourself is, too.
13. Cut toxic people out of your life. The longer you keep them, the more harm they'll do.

14. You are enough, and your feelings are valid. Don't let anyone tell you otherwise.
15. Don't stay with someone toxic just because you have a history with them. Let them go.
16. If you're in a relationship and cry more than you smile, you're with the wrong person.
17. Telling someone to stay positive all the time is really bad advice.
18. You'll still have a great life, even if you don't get into your dream college.

Diary of an Anxious Girl.

Hey there. Whoever is reading this, I hope you're doing fine, not overthinking about things that don't even matter, choosing people who choose you, and taking care of yourself.

Now, coming to my story.

Who am I? I'm just an adult who used to overthink.

In 2016, some incidents happened. Just like every other student, I took my phone to school but wasn't lucky enough to not get caught.

Some shit happened, and it became a big deal.

All of the teachers and students turned their backs on me.

That's when my journey of 'not giving a fuck' started.

Not only students but teachers also talked shit about me.

It was hard for me, really hard.

I was just in 8th grade. I didn't know how to handle all this hate.

I used to get scolded all the time, even when it wasn't my fault.

Teachers would tell kids not to hang out with me.

I always used to wonder what I had done to deserve this.

It hurt so much that one day, it stopped hurting. I stopped caring about what they said. I realised that my life was too short to spend it thinking about what other people had to say about me.

I got used to being alone.

I started liking my company.

I realised that I've only got myself at the end of the day.

I realised that no matter what, anyone can leave you regardless of the promises they make. And it's okay because you don't need anyone to make you feel happy.

I didn't know what was happening or what I was going to do, but I didn't give up. I survived because that's what you got to do in this life. Abuse isn't only physical.

My friends told me everything about our relationship was wrong, yet I was blinded by what I thought was love.

I used to cry more than I used to smile. I wasn't living; I was just surviving, but the worst part was that I didn't know I was being abused when it happened to me.

Everyone said the same thing: Why didn't you leave him before? No one understands that it wasn't easy. That abuse was full of pain, manipulation, and gaslighting. But that abuse, for sure, didn't last forever. It made me realise my worth and made me strong.

Little did I know that the boy I thought was perfect for me, would abuse me emotionally. I used to wonder how I let myself get to that point.

The truth is, it starts slowly. At first, when it happens, you're just like, 'Oh, it's okay. He apologised and said it won't happen again.'

But it does happen again. The cycle continues, and before you know it; you're crying every single day and wondering what went wrong.

He turned out to be everything I never thought he would be. Everyone warned me about him, but I fought for him. As it turned out, everyone was right.

It was one of the hardest battles I've fought, but I came out so much stronger than before.

Sometimes, you have to go through pain to be happy.

The times that you feel you won't get over something; remember that time will heal everything.

If you're reading this and can say you're in the same situation, please get yourself out of it.

Love, you deserve so much better.

Dogs.

The best creation of god.

Those who love unconditionally.

They are these beautiful creatures who will love you till the day they die and expect nothing in return.

They are so effortlessly beautiful that it almost makes me cry as I write this.

It breaks my heart when I hear about people hurting them, not people; they are monsters who feed themselves by being cruel to the most innocent creatures of nature.

If I could, I would take away all their sorrows and pain, and claim them as mine. I'd give them nothing but pure love and happiness, even if it means I'd have to be in pain throughout.

Whenever I see animal cruelty, all I can think about is: Why? What did that sweet baby do to you? What was that innocent creature's fault? And to think that people do this for fun, for amusement; it makes my blood boil as hot as lava.

Please be kind to them.

They can't speak for themselves, but we can. If you can't help, please don't hurt them.

The 'everyone's doing so well' anxiety.

The thoughts of everyone else doing great at life, being so happy, and having it all figured out makes me scared. Don't get me wrong; I'm happy for them but scared for myself. I'm afraid that I am not going to achieve that happiness. Am I going to be able to achieve my goals?

Sometimes, I hate social media; for it shows the best of everyone's life. It makes other people feel shitty about themselves. But then again, not everything people show on social media is true.

The thought of not achieving greatness, whether in my life, relationships, or career, gives me crippling anxiety and keeps me up at night. Writing this at four in the morning proved it well. But after a few hours of panic, I eventually realised it was okay. Everyone's timeline is not the same. I'll achieve success when it's my time and I trust myself. When my time comes; it will be a hell lot of amazing.

What makes me proud of myself is that even if I could be anyone in the world, I'd still choose to be who I am right now. You are you; that's your power, and nothing or nobody can change it. Embrace yourself, and be the person you always wanted to be.

Be kind.

Do you know what goes inside a person's mind? No, you don't. So, who are you to make any assumptions? People with depression aren't lazy. People with anxiety aren't crazy. People who visit a therapist aren't insane.

Do you know why people feel alone? It is because of the discrimination of mental health. They are afraid to open up, share their problems, and get help. Sometimes, it's their parents who don't take them seriously or students who mock them. Mental health is just as important as physical health. In my opinion, mental health is the top priority. No matter what you do in life, does it all matter if you aren't happy?

Your healing is about you; you don't need anyone's approval. It's all about you.

You have the right to acknowledge your feelings without having to justify them.

You are not alone in this. People start to heal the moment they are heard. One of the best ways to heal is to get everything out.

A little more kindness, a little less judgement.

Be kind, people. Sometimes, your help can save someone's life.

Think before you speak. You have no idea how much your words can hurt someone.

Mental health matters.

Why is moving on so important?

Moving on from people, from places, from memories.

You can never forget the memories people gave you, but you can sure as hell move on from them.

You need to move on from your past so that your future can be clear.

You need to let go of things that you cling to just to make yourself feel good, because how else will you be able to achieve what god has in store for you in the future?

Let go of that toxic relationship or friendship.

Let go of that person who gives you temporary happiness but harms you in the long run.

Not even a single day goes by when I don't think of achieving everything I've dreamt of. Some things keep me up at night, and some give me chills when I think about having the life I have always envisioned. One day, I'll have it all. One day, I'll fulfil all my dreams. One day, I'll fall for someone who'll fall for me too. One day, my parents will be proud of me.

Each one of us experiences numerous things, that makes us realise life is indeed too short. Anything can happen, so whenever you get to tell your loved ones that you love them, don't hesitate. Whenever you get an opportunity to do something you love, do it.

Take the year 2020 for instance. A year so full of surprises. One of the biggest things we learnt from the year Covid-19 hit us was being more resilient, more patient, and fighting our battles head-on. From being quarantined and isolated, to the world gradually opening up; somewhere in-between I know you felt alone. It felt like you had no one to talk to, but know that you weren't alone. We were all in the same boat.

Sometimes, life presents unusual circumstances in front of us. But when we choose to be strong and face them, we get through it come what may. Remember, there's nothing you can't do. There's nothing you can't achieve, once you put your mind to it.

The pandemic taught us that just like good times don't last forever, bad times too do not last forever. The challenges we face too shall pass not because they're momentary, but because they're here to teach us valuable lessons and learning from them is a constant part of our life.

Happiness

Happiness for me is coming back home from a shopping trip. It feels like my heart is full.

It's only for a while, but I feel like I have everything in the world.

All of the things that I bought somehow make me so happy.

Happiness is when I'm about to take the first bite of my favourite meal while watching my favourite show on Netflix.

Happiness is also letting go.

Letting go of someone toxic in your life, who doesn't encourage or support you.

I had this feeling when I removed someone really toxic from my life, and their actions stopped affecting me. That was amazing.

Trust me, letting go and moving on from someone who makes you feel you aren't enough is the best thing to do.

You deserve someone who supports you and your dreams, someone who won't give up on you.

Stop using love as an excuse for tolerating disrespect.

Let go of all the toxicity. God has something beautiful planned for all of us.

That feeling,

When you know you're about to cry, the way your throat starts to burn, your nose turns red, and you begin to tremble. It's not so great, isn't it?

But sometimes, crying is good. Let it all out.

Pain deserves to be felt.

Love.

Yes, it's beautiful but only when you're with the right person.

No, love does not suck, relationships aren't shit.

It's all about the person.

Yes, many of us have a bad opinion about relationships and love because of one person.

That one person who cheated on us, who hurt us, who turned our smiles into tears.

To all the people suffering,

I want to let you know that someday, someone will love you so much that smiling will hurt your face.

Just because one person hurt you or cheated on you doesn't mean everyone will.

Darling, your priority should be you and only you.

The person who truly loves you will support you and your goals, trust you, be there for you, sometimes fight with you, but most importantly, love you unconditionally.

Putting restrictions on someone isn't love; trusting them is.

Love should have the fear of losing someone, not the fear of doing something that your partner wouldn't like.

Love is when someone accepts you for who you are and won't ask you to change.

There's a difference between protecting and controlling someone; everyone should know it.

Love shouldn't be about getting revenge. Love is when you choose not to hurt the person, even when you have all the opportunity in the world to do so.

When she dies,

She doesn't want to be remembered for her last moments, her last words, or what other people perceived her as.

She wants to be remembered for who she actually was.

For changing her life and that of others as well.

She wishes to be remembered for the way she used to love unconditionally.

For the way she never used to give up, no matter how hard it got.

For her way of living and surviving, when surviving was the only option she had left.

For smiling and never letting her crown down even when everything was going to hell in her life.

Most importantly, I appreciate how she helped others when she couldn't help herself.

THIRTEEN

To Those Who Hurt Me

THANK YOU.

For trying to break me. (You actually thought you'd be successful? Now that's just cocky.)

For making me feel like I wasn't enough, because you taught me how to prove that I am.

You gave me pain.

I turned it into a purpose.

You tried to silence me.

I wrote a book instead.

I don't forgive you, I outgrew you, and **while you keep talking, I'll be going places.**

Instead of hurting other people, maybe go and do something meaningful in your life, maybe you could learn a little something, I guess?

Anyhow, all the best to you, may you learn how to be a better person.

FOURTEEN

Write Your Own Story Now

DEAR READER, IF YOU ARE STRUGGLING RIGHT NOW, let me tell you, you will be okay. You will figure things out and control how it turns out.

As actor Ranbir Kapoor's character Ved said in *Tamasha*: '*Ending Sahi Nahi Hai? Koi Baat Nahi, Apni Kahani Hai. Ending Badal Denge!*'

'Is the ending not quite right? It doesn't matter—after all, it's my story. I'll change the ending!'

So, you too go ahead and change that ending, this is your chance.

Don't let anyone stop you or silence you.

It's your life, you deserve to live it the way you want to.

All of us want to heal, but we don't know how to. Social media fools us every day while showing us an aesthetic world that doesn't really exist.

Maybe healing doesn't look like sunshine and flowers.

Maybe it's waking up and deciding to try again.

Maybe it's crying on the bathroom floor at 2 a.m. and still showing up the next morning.

Maybe it's whispering 'I'm still here' even when the world feels like too much.

I used to think I had to be strong all the time. That I had to hide the broken parts, patch them up with a smile, and pretend nothing ever happened. But I was wrong.

I've been through hell, and not the kind people always see.

I've felt hands that shouldn't have touched me.

I've heard words that hurt deeper than a knife.

I've been bullied for just being me.

I've battled the heaviness of depression that made even breathing feel like a chore.

I've stared at the ceiling with tears, wondering if the world would be better without me in it.

And I've grieved my best friend, whom I loved with everything in me, people who are no longer here but live on in every heartbeat, every sentence I write.

But through it all, I've learned something no one teaches you:

Pain doesn't make you weak, it makes you human.

Survival isn't just existing, it's choosing to keep going, again and again, when nothing makes sense.

There were days I didn't want to be here. Days when the weight of it all felt impossible. But I stayed. I fought. I let myself fall apart. And slowly, piece by piece, I began to rebuild.

This book is proof that even the most shattered souls can find light again.

Not in some magical, perfect way.

But in the small things:

In laughter that returns unexpectedly.

In friends who sit with you in silence.

In therapy sessions that hurt but heal.

In choosing yourself, even when it's hard.

In realising that your story, all of it, matters.

So, my dear reader,

You are not alone.

Not in your pain. Not in your darkness. Not in your slow journey back to life.

It's okay not to be okay.

It's okay to take time. To scream, cry, and feel everything too deeply.

It's okay to rest. To start over. To choose yourself.

What's not okay is giving up on yourself, losing your self-respect over someone who doesn't deserve you.

You're not broken. You're becoming.

And the world is better with you in it.

FIFTEEN

Finding Myself

TO BE HONEST, I AM STILL TRYING TO FIND MYSELF. One thing I have realised after watching director Imtiaz Ali's masterpiece, *Tamasha* (over a 100 times), is that I relate way too much to the character, Ved. I remember thinking, 'The same story, the same pain; how long will it go on for? What about my happy ending?' It felt like life was stuck on repeat, and something had to change. It was high time I found myself again. I loved writing, and I knew I had the talent, so why not show it to the world? What's the worst that could happen? Maybe people wouldn't relate to it, and that's okay. Everyone's story is different.

This is my story, and I want to make sure my ending is the right one. And if it doesn't feel right, so what? It's my story, I can always change the ending.

After going through bullying, heartbreaks, depression, and anxiety, I often wondered whether these experiences would make me or break me. But then I thought, why not turn this pain into art? At least something good might come out of all the tears I've shed.

So, one day, I finally did what my heart wanted.

I was exhausted from scrolling through Instagram, watching everyone live their best lives as I felt stuck. I remember thinking, 'This is it. I can't do this anymore.' So with an anxious mind but an excited heart, I submitted my resignation letter.

But once the rush faded, reality hit me. In the excitement of following my passion, I had quit my job… but now what?

What if I fail?

Then again, how would I ever know if I don't try? I would rather try and fail, than live a life full of regrets.

So, if your life ever feels like it's falling apart, or you feel stuck in an impossible situation, remember: It will all be okay.

Because sometimes, it's okay not to be okay.

To Everyone Facing Struggles Right Now

I CAN'T RECALL HOW MANY TIMES I'VE FELT ALONE AND unloved. Sometimes, I would cry so loudly, that I would have to put my hand on my mouth so that no one would hear. Because if someone did, I wouldn't be able to explain and even if I did, they wouldn't understand. I don't know how many times I wanted to take my own life, end the pain once and for all, thinking that no one would even care if I disappeared.

I begged god for the pain to stop because I couldn't take it anymore. At one point, I gave up. Whatever god put in front of me, I kept on facing it. All the things that happened to me, eventually made me stronger.

I remember rushing to the washroom whenever I had a panic attack so that my parents wouldn't know. I remember being numb from the pain; I wouldn't stop shaking, sweating and crying. I couldn't sleep or eat.

However, things started getting better with time and more awareness.

It was a moment of realisation for me. You have to go through pain to achieve happiness. Life won't always be good, but it won't be bad forever. Bad things happen but you have to go through them and live your life.

Sometimes, when things look like the end of the world, know that you will survive. You'll be fine, and sometime later you'll think about it and see how strong you've become.

In the end, everything will be fine because if it's not, then it's not the end.

Please don't be afraid to get help. You will thank yourself.

Thank you, not just for reading my book but for reading my life's story.

Even if a part of this book helped you feel seen, heard, or healed, then my work here is done.

Stay true to who you are instead of pretending to be someone else. Trust me, you will be happier.

Always remember to be yourself, as it's better to live a life full of experiences rather than a life full of regrets. It's okay to be you, okay?

To be continued....

—Ghanishta

Acknowledgements

I would like to express my love and gratitude to those who have supported me throughout this journey.

I want to thank my parents, for their unwavering love, encouragement, belief and support throughout. Papa, thank you for making every single one of my demands and wishes come true.

Coco senior, even though you were in my life for 5 months, the love you gave me will last a lifetime. Thank you.

I owe a great deal of this book to my personal experiences, and I am very proud to have never given up on myself, even when life seemed too difficult.

Lastly, I want to thank every reader—for trusting me with your time and for allowing my words to be a part of your journey.

To everyone who has faced mental health struggles, this book is for you. Your courage inspires me every day, and I hope these words provide you with the comfort, strength, and hope you need.

Remember, it's okay to seek help.

About the Author

Ghanishta Khosla is a passionate writer, a strong advocate for mental health, and a firm believer in the power of self-love and self-improvement. She possesses a background in creative writing along with a personal connection to writing; speaking from her personal experiences in the topics of mental health, relationships, and teenage life. Ghanishta has dedicated her writing to creating safe spaces for readers to explore their feelings, heal, and grow. When not writing, she dreams about making the world a better place through her writings, travelling, and living a life that blends creativity, adventure, and meaningful connections.

About the Author

[illegible]